Graphic Design

Stunning Visuals

or monetary loss due to the information herein, either directly or indirectly.

Table of content

Chapter 1: Introduction to Graphic Design

Graphic design is a powerful tool for communication. It is the art of creating visual content to communicate a message or idea. Graphic design is used across all industries to create logos, brochures, websites, posters, and more.

Graphic design is a complex process that requires an understanding of color, composition, typography, and layout. A successful graphic designer must be able to interpret a client's brief and create visuals that are visually appealing and convey the intended message.

Graphic design is an ever-evolving field. Technology has enabled graphic designers to create visuals that were not possible a few decades ago. New software and tools are constantly being developed to make creating visuals easier.

In this book, you will learn the basics of graphic design. You will learn about the fundamentals of color, composition, typography, and layout and how to use them to create stunning visuals. We will also discuss different tools and software available to make the process of creating visuals easier.

You will also learn how to create logos, websites, posters, and brochures. You will learn how to develop a concept and bring it to life with visuals. You will also learn how to work with clients to ensure their vision is met.

Finally, you will learn how to market yourself as a graphic designer. You will learn how to promote your work, build a portfolio, and find clients. You will also learn how to set up a pricing structure and how to manage projects.

By the end of this book, you will have a thorough understanding of graphic design and be ready to create stunning visuals. So, let's begin our journey into the world of graphic design!

Chapter 2: Learning the Basics of Graphic Design

Now that the basics of graphic design have been introduced, it is time to delve into the fundamentals. Graphic design is a skill that requires learning and practice to master. It is important to familiarize oneself with the tools of the trade and understand how to use them effectively.

The first step in learning the basics of graphic design is to understand the principles of design. These principles include balance, contrast, hierarchy, alignment, repetition, and proximity. These principles are fundamental to creating effective visuals that are aesthetically pleasing and communicate the intended message.

Once the fundamentals of design are understood, the next step is to familiarize oneself with the tools of graphic design. These tools include software programs such as Adobe Photoshop, Illustrator, and InDesign. Additionally, it is important to understand how to use the various tools within the software programs, such as selecting and manipulating objects, working with layers, and using colors and typography to create visual impact.

In addition to learning the software programs, it is also important to understand the fundamentals of composition. This includes understanding how to create a pleasing layout, how to use whitespace effectively, and how to create a hierarchy of information. It is also important to become familiar with the different types of images and how to manipulate them for the desired effect.

As one progresses in their understanding of graphic design, it is important to become familiar with the various trends and styles. This includes understanding the different graphic design styles such as minimalism, modernism, and vintage. Additionally, one should also be familiar with more specialized techniques such as logo design, web design, and infographics.

Finally, it is important to understand how to apply the principles of design in a practical way. This includes understanding how to create effective visuals that are visually appealing and communicate the desired message. Additionally, it is important to understand how to create visuals that are consistent and cohesive across different platforms.

By taking the time to learn the basics of graphic design, one can develop the skills needed to create stunning visuals that effectively communicate their message. With practice and dedication, anyone can become a proficient graphic designer.

2.1: Design Principles

The art of graphic design requires creative thinking and a keen eye for detail. When constructing visuals, it is important to have a set of design principles to guide the process. Design principles are the fundamental concepts, rules, and guidelines used to create aesthetically pleasing visuals. These principles provide a framework for constructing visuals that are well-balanced, visually appealing, and meaningful.

The following are some of the most important design principles to consider when creating visuals:

Balance: Balance is the distribution of elements across a visual in a way that creates a sense of equilibrium. It is important to consider how elements such as color, shape, size, and texture interact with each other.

Contrast: Contrast is the juxtaposition of elements that creates an interesting visual effect. Contrast can be achieved through the use of color, shape, size, and texture.

Hierarchy: Hierarchy is the way elements are arranged in order of importance. By assigning different levels of importance to elements, it becomes easier to create a visually pleasing visual.

Unity: Unity is the overall feeling of cohesion that is achieved when elements are combined harmoniously. It is important to consider how individual elements interact with one another to create a unified whole.

Proportion: Proportion is the relationship between the size of elements. It is important to consider the size of elements in relation to each other when constructing visuals.

Rhythm: Rhythm is the repetition of elements that creates a visual pattern. By repeating elements, it is possible to create a sense of movement or energy.

Emphasis: Emphasis is the focal point of a visual. It is important to consider where the emphasis of a visual should be placed in order to create an effective visual.

These design principles are essential for creating visuals that are visually appealing. By following these principles, it is possible to create visuals that are well-balanced, aesthetically pleasing, and meaningful.

2.2: Types of Graphic Design

Graphic design is an ever-evolving field with a variety of styles and approaches. Knowing which type of design suits a project best can be a challenge, but is an essential part of creating a successful outcome. This section will provide a brief overview of the various types of graphic design and their uses.

Vector Graphic Design is a type of design that uses geometric shapes, curves, and lines to create illustrations. Vector graphics are ideal for creating logos, icons, and illustrations as they provide a clean, sharp look. Vector graphics are also highly scalable, meaning they can be resized with no loss of quality.

Raster Graphic Design uses pixels to create images and is the most common type of graphic design. It is used to create photographs, illustrations, and complex designs. Raster graphics are not as sharp or clean as vector graphics and are not as easily scaled without a loss of quality.

3D Graphic Design is a type of design that uses three-dimensional objects and scenes to create visuals. 3D graphics are often used for product design, motion graphics, and architectural visualizations. 3D graphics are highly detailed and require a high level of skill and knowledge to create.

Motion Graphic Design uses animation, video, and sound to create visuals that move. It is used to create videos, explainer videos, and short films. Motion graphics are often used to create captivating visuals that tell a story.

Print Graphic Design is a type of design that focuses on creating visuals for print. It is often used to create flyers, posters, brochures, magazines, and other printed materials. Print design requires a good understanding of printing processes and materials to ensure the highest quality outcome.

Interactive Graphic Design is a type of design that focuses on creating visuals for digital platforms. It is used to create websites, mobile apps, and games. Interactive design requires a good understanding of user experience and user interface design to ensure a positive experience for users.

Graphic design is a vast and complex field with many approaches and styles. Knowing which type of design is best suited for a project can be the difference between success and failure. This section provided a brief overview of the various types of graphic design and their uses. With a better understanding of the different types of design available, designers can create stunning visuals that are both visually appealing and effective.

2.3: Choosing Colors

When it comes to graphic design, choosing the right colors can make or break the final product. It is important to understand how color works in order to create stunning visuals. As such, this will give an overview of how to choose the best colors for your design.

First and foremost, it is important to understand the basics of color theory. This includes understanding the color wheel, the different hues and tints of colors, and the impact of warm and cool colors. Once you understand the basics, you can begin to experiment with different combinations of colors to create the desired effect.

When choosing which colors to use, it is important to consider the context of the design. For example, if the design is for a children's book, then brighter and more vibrant colors may be appropriate. If the design is for a corporate website, then more neutral colors may be best.

It is also important to consider the message that the colors are trying to convey. If you are trying to convey a sense of energy and excitement, then brighter colors may be the way to go. If you are trying to create a sense of calm and relaxation, then softer, cooler colors may be best.

Finally, when choosing colors, it is important to consider the relationship between the colors. Complimentary colors, such as red and green, can be used to create a vibrant and dynamic look. Analogous colors, such as blue and green, can be used to create a more subtle and calming look.

Choosing the right colors for your graphic design is essential for creating stunning visuals. By understanding the basics of color theory, considering the context of the design, and considering the relationship between colors, you can create the desired effect and ensure that your design stands out.

Chapter 3: Understanding the Design Process

Graphic design is a powerful medium for communicating ideas. It has the potential to create stunning visuals that capture the attention of viewers and convey a message. To be successful, designers must understand the design process from start to finish. In this chapter, readers will learn the essential elements of the design process and how to use them to create effective designs.

The first step in the design process is to define the project's purpose and objectives. This includes identifying the target audience, determining the overall look and feel, and establishing the scope of the project. Once the objectives are established, the designer can move on to the next step: research. Research involves exploring the client's needs, gathering data, and gathering inspiration from other sources.

After the research stage is completed, the designer can begin the concept development process. This includes brainstorming ideas, sketching out potential solutions, and refining the concepts. Once the concept is finalized, the designer can move on to the next step: creating a design brief. A design brief is a document that outlines the project's objectives, deliverables, timeline, cost, and any other relevant information.

The next step is to create the visual elements of the design. This includes selecting colors, fonts, and other visual elements. It's important to keep the target audience in mind when selecting these elements. Once the elements are chosen, the designer can assemble them into a cohesive design. This is known as the layout phase.

After the layout is complete, the designer can move on to the refinement phase. This includes making adjustments to the design to ensure it meets the project's objectives. This includes making sure the design is aesthetically pleasing, that the elements are positioned appropriately, and that the overall design is cohesive.

Finally, the designer can move on to the production phase. This includes preparing the design for printing or web production. This includes ensuring that the elements are the correct size and format, that the colors are accurate, and that all links and navigation are functioning properly.

By understanding the design process from start to finish, designers can create effective and appealing designs that communicate the intended message. In the next chapter, readers will learn how to use design software to create stunning visuals.

3.1: Brainstorming

Brainstorming is an effective method for generating ideas. It allows designers to explore a wide range of possibilities, come up with creative solutions, and identify potential problems. It is an important step in the design process, as it allows designers to think through their ideas and develop them in a structured way.

Brainstorming can be done in a variety of ways. It can be done alone, with a team, or in a group setting. It is important to note that it is not a matter of coming up with the best solution, but rather creating an environment in which ideas can be explored and explored further.

When brainstorming, it is essential to remain open-minded. It is important to consider all ideas, no matter how seemingly outrageous. This can help to generate a range of ideas that may not have been immediately thought of.

It is also essential to think outside the box. This means to look beyond the obvious and obvious solutions to find something new and creative. This is a great way to create visuals that stand out from the crowd.

When brainstorming, it is important to be as organized as possible. It is helpful to create a list of topics or questions that can be explored. This can help to keep the brainstorming session focused and ensure that all ideas are explored.

It is also important to keep the conversation flowing. This means to ask questions, make suggestions, and encourage participation. This ensures that everyone is involved in the session, allowing for more ideas to be generated.

Finally, it is important to record the ideas generated during the brainstorming session. This can be done in a variety of ways, such as using post-it notes, writing on a whiteboard, or using a computer program. This ensures that all ideas are documented and can be referred to later.

Brainstorming is an important step in the design process. It allows designers to explore a wide range of possibilities, come up with creative solutions, and identify potential problems. By remaining open-minded, thinking outside the box, being organized, and recording ideas, designers can ensure that their design process is as effective as possible.

3.2: Sketching

Sketching is a fundamental part of the graphic design process. It provides designers with the opportunity to quickly explore ideas and experiment with layouts. Sketches are an effective way to communicate ideas and concepts, and they are often used to present design work to clients.

For the novice designer, sketching can seem intimidating. However, with practice, it can become an invaluable tool. Before sketching, it is important to develop a plan. Consider the purpose of the design, the target audience, and the desired outcome. This will help to guide the design process.

When sketching, it is important to start with simple shapes. This will help to create a structure for the design. Start by sketching basic geometric shapes, such as rectangles, circles, and triangles. Once the basic structure is in place, the designer can begin to add details.

To capture the desired effect, it is important to use a variety of mediums. Pencils, markers, and colored pencils can all be used to express different ideas. Using a variety of mediums can help to create a more dynamic design.

When sketching, it is important to limit the number of details included. Too many details can make the design look cluttered and overwhelming. Instead, focus on the main elements of the design.

When presenting the design to a client, it is important to include sketches as part of the presentation. This will help to demonstrate the concept and explain the design process. By including sketches, the designer will be able to demonstrate their thought process and their ability to create effective designs.

Sketching is an important part of the graphic design process. It is an effective way to explore ideas and communicate concepts. With practice, sketching can become a powerful tool for any designer.

3.3: Refining

Graphic design professionals understand the importance of refining their work. Every design should be taken through a comprehensive review process to evaluate its effectiveness and to ensure that it meets the client's requirements. Refining can be a time consuming process, but it is essential to produce a quality product.

The first step in refining a design is to review it for accuracy. Ensure that all the elements are in the correct place, that the text is legible, and that the colors are correctly chosen. If there are any errors, these should be corrected before proceeding further.

The second step is to evaluate the design from a usability perspective. Does the design provide the user with the information they need? Are the navigation options clear and intuitive? Consider the user experience when refining the design and make changes as necessary.

Next, consider the aesthetics of the design. Are the colors and fonts pleasing to the eye? Does the overall design flow well together? Make adjustments to the color palette and font selection if needed.

Finally, look at the technical aspects of the design. Is the file size appropriate? Are the resolution and image quality at the required level? Make sure all aspects of the design are technically sound before submitting it to the client.

Refining a design takes time and effort, but it is essential for producing a quality end product. Take the time to review and adjust the design until it is perfect. The extra effort will pay off in the long run and result in a design that is both effective and aesthetically pleasing.

3.4: Testing

is an important step in the graphic design process. It ensures that the visuals created are of the highest quality and meet the needs of the client or project. Testing also allows the designer to identify any potential problems or issues that may arise during the creation process.

Testing can be done in several ways, including user testing, usability testing, and A/B testing. User testing involves testing the visuals on a group of people to assess how they interact with the visuals. This can help to identify any areas of improvement or potential problems. Usability testing measures how easy it is for a user to use the visuals, and A/B testing compares two versions of a visual to determine which one is more effective.

It is important to ensure that the testing is done in a controlled environment. This means that the same conditions, such as the same device or platform, must be used for all tests. Additionally, it is important to ensure that the test subjects are representative of the target audience for the visuals.

Testing should be conducted regularly throughout the design process. This allows the designer to make any necessary adjustments as the project progresses. It also ensures that the visuals are meeting the needs of the client or project.

The results of the testing should be carefully evaluated. It is important to consider how the results could affect the visuals. Additionally, it is important to note any potential problems that were identified during the testing.

Testing is an important step in the graphic design process. It allows the designer to identify any potential problems or issues that may arise. Additionally, it ensures that the visuals created are of the highest quality and meet the needs of the client or project. Testing should be conducted regularly throughout the design process and the results should be carefully evaluated to ensure the success of the visuals.

Chapter 4: Creating Digital Art

Digital art is becoming increasingly popular as a creative outlet. With the help of various digital tools and software, artists are able to create unique, intricate pieces of art that can be shared with the world. This chapter will delve into the process of creating digital art, from the basics of how to get started to the more advanced techniques and tips for bringing your art to life.

First, it is important to understand the basics of digital art. There are several different types of programs and tools used for creating digital art. Some of the most popular programs used by digital artists include Adobe Photoshop, Illustrator, and Corel Painter. These programs provide a variety of features and tools, allowing for a wide range of creative possibilities. Additionally, there are a number of free and open-source programs available, such as GIMP and Krita, that are also suitable for creating digital art.

Once you have chosen the program you wish to use, the next step is to familiarize yourself with the program's tools and features. Most digital art programs come with tutorials and guides to help get you started. Additionally, there are a number of online tutorials and resources available to help you learn how to use the program. Taking the time to understand how to use the software is essential for creating successful digital art.

Once you have become familiar with the program, you can begin to create your artwork. Many digital artists find it helpful to start with a sketch or idea of what they want to create. This can be done either on paper or digitally in the program. Then, you can begin to add layers and add color to your artwork. It is also important to remember to save your work frequently, as digital art files can be easily corrupted.

When creating digital art, it is important to remember to not be afraid to experiment. Digital art is an iterative process, so don't be afraid to try something new and see what happens. Additionally, it is important to remember that digital art programs are meant to be used as a tool, not a crutch. Ultimately, the artist is responsible for the final product.

Finally, once you have completed your artwork, it is important to understand how to share it with the world. You will need to export your digital art in a format that can be easily shared, such as a JPEG, PNG, or PDF. Additionally, there are a number of websites and platforms that allow for digital art to be displayed and shared.

This chapter has provided an overview of how to create digital art. With the right tools and knowledge, anyone can create stunning visuals. Digital art is an exciting form of expression, and with the right tools and techniques, you can create artwork that will be admired by many.

4.1: Digital Painting

Digital painting is an art form that enables designers to create stunning visuals with a digital canvas. It is the process of using digital tools to create art in the same way traditional painting would be done with a brush, pencil, or other traditional art media. Digital painting can be used to create imaginative illustrations, concept art, and illustrations for books and magazines.

Digital painting is becoming increasingly popular among designers due to the ease of use and the array of digital tools available. With digital painting, designers are able to produce work quickly and accurately. Furthermore, digital painting can be achieved on a variety of platforms, such as tablets, laptops, and smartphones.

Designers can choose from a range of digital painting tools, including brushes, pencils, markers, and shapes. These tools can be used in combination with other design tools to create dynamic visuals. Designers also have the ability to adjust the size, shape, and color of the paint strokes. Additionally, they can utilize layers to create depth and texture for the painting.

Designers are also able to make use of digital painting software. This software allows designers to experiment with different brushes, colors, and textures to create unique visuals. Designers are able to save their work, so they can be revisited and edited later. Additionally, this software allows designers to share their work with others online.

Finally, designers are able to use digital painting techniques to create animations. By using a combination of layers and brushes, designers can create aesthetically pleasing animations. Furthermore, with digital painting, designers can create backgrounds for videos and animations.

Digital painting has become an essential skill for graphic designers. By mastering digital painting techniques, designers are able to create stunning visuals with ease. As technology continues to evolve, designers are able to use this skill to create even more dynamic visuals.

4.2: Digital Drawing

Digital drawing is a powerful tool for graphic designers. It enables them to create stunning visuals with accuracy and precision. With digital drawing, graphic designers can produce artwork with a variety of features, such as layering, effects, and shapes. Digital drawing also allows for color correction and manipulation, making it an essential tool for creating visually stunning images and designs.

The most popular type of digital drawing is vector drawing. Vector drawing uses mathematical equations to create art and graphics, giving graphic designers the ability to create detailed and intricate designs. Vector drawing is also highly scalable, meaning it can be used for both small and large scale projects.

Raster drawing is another type of digital drawing. This type of drawing uses a grid of pixels to create art and graphics. Raster drawing is not as precise as vector drawing, however, it is more suited to creating illustrations and complex photos. Raster drawing is also used for creating textures and patterns.

Digital drawing programs typically come with a variety of features and tools. These tools can help graphic designers to create detailed visuals and artwork quickly and easily. Common features include layers, brushes, selection tools, and color swatches. Many digital drawing programs also offer filters and effects, which can be used to add additional depth and dimension to artwork.

When creating digital artwork, it is important to keep in mind the size of the project. Digital drawing programs can be used for projects of any size, however, it is important to consider the resolution of the artwork. If the artwork is to be used in a print format, the resolution should be set to a higher resolution. On the other hand, if the artwork is to be used on the web, the resolution should be set to a lower resolution.

Digital drawing is a powerful tool for graphic designers. With it, they can create stunning visuals with accuracy and precision. Vector and raster drawing are the two most popular types of digital drawing, and both offer a variety of features and tools to help graphic designers create detailed artwork quickly and easily. Before beginning a digital drawing project, it is important to consider the size and resolution of the artwork.

4.3: Digital Typography

Digital typography is a form of graphic design that deals with the arrangement, presentation, and appearance of text. It is an essential component of effective graphic design, as it impacts the overall readability, legibility, and impact of the visual design. Digital typography can involve a wide range of techniques, from basic type manipulation to more complex font and layout design.

Designers use digital typography to create visually appealing and readable text for a variety of purposes, such as webpages, books, posters, and advertisements. The foundational elements of digital typography include font selection, size, contrast, spacing, and layout. With digital typography, designers can create harmonious and engaging visuals that are both aesthetically pleasing and easy to read.

Font selection is one of the most important aspects of digital typography. The right font can create an impactful message or evoke a desired emotion. When selecting a font, designers should consider its readability, size, and style. Fonts can range from decorative and unique to simple and classic, and there are a variety of typefaces available to fit any design need.

Size is another important element of digital typography. It determines the prominence of the text and how well it communicates its message. Generally, larger fonts are easier to read, while smaller fonts can be more effective for titles or headings. When selecting a size, it's important to consider the context of the text and the size of the page or screen.

Contrast is also an important factor in digital typography. The contrast between the text and the background should be high enough to ensure that the text is legible. It's also important to consider the contrast between the font size and the font weight.

Spacing is a critical part of digital typography and can impact the readability of the text. Proper spacing helps separate the elements of the design and makes the text easier to read. Designers should pay attention to the size and spacing of the letters, words, and lines, as well as the white space between elements.

Layout is the final element of digital typography. It refers to the arrangement of the text on the page or screen. Designers should consider the size of the page, the number of columns, and the placement of the text. The layout should be organized, consistent, and easy to navigate.

Digital typography is an essential component of effective graphic design. By understanding the fundamentals of font selection, size, contrast, spacing, and layout, designers can create visually appealing and readable text for a variety of projects.

Chapter 5: Working with Photos and Images

Graphic design is an art form that requires creativity, but it also needs technical knowledge. In this chapter, we will discuss the basics of working with photos and images. We will learn how to prepare photos for use in graphic design projects, how to manipulate images to create stunning visuals, and how to use images to convey a message.

The first step when working with photos and images is to prepare them for use in a graphic design project. This involves optimizing the size and resolution of the image and ensuring that it is suitable for the project. Images should be scaled to the correct size to ensure they look as sharp and detailed as possible. If the image is too large, it can be resized and compressed to reduce file size without sacrificing quality.

Once the photo or image is ready for use, it can be manipulated to create a stunning visual. This could include adding text, changing the colors, or cropping the image. Many graphic design programs offer tools to help with these adjustments, but it is important to understand the fundamentals of design and composition to make the most of these tools.

Image manipulation can also be used to create a visual representation of a concept or message. This could involve blending multiple photos or images together to create a unique image. Or it could involve adding elements to create a custom graphic. Imagery can be used to convey a powerful message, and graphic designers must understand how to use these tools to create stunning visuals.

Finally, it is important to understand how to use images to communicate effectively. This could involve choosing images that support the overall message or theme of the project. It could also involve optimizing images for different platforms, such as websites or print. Understanding how to use images in the most effective way is an important skill for any graphic designer.

In conclusion, working with photos and images is an essential part of graphic design. From preparing images for use to creating visuals to communicate a message, it is important to understand the fundamentals of working with photos and images. With the right tools and knowledge, graphic designers can create stunning visuals that will capture the attention of their audience.

5.1: Photo Editing

Photo editing is one of the most important aspects of graphic design and can help transform a photo into a stunning visual. This provides an overview of the various techniques used in photo editing.

The first step in photo editing is to acquire the photo. This can be done through a digital camera, scanner, stock photo library, or the internet. Once the image has been acquired, the next step is to prepare the image for editing. This includes cropping the photo to its desired size and resolution, as well as adjusting the color and contrast of the image.

Next, the photo editor can use various tools to make adjustments to the photo. These tools can help enhance the colors, reduce noise, sharpen the image, and more. Some of the more advanced tools can also be used to create special effects, such as blurring, adding light and shadow, and creating texture.

The photo editor can also apply various filters to the photo. Filters can be used to change the look and feel of the photo, such as adding a vintage effect, giving the photo a dreamy look, or creating a black and white photo.

The photo editor can also use text and other graphic elements to enhance the photo. This can be done by adding captions, text overlays, logos, and a variety of other graphic elements.

Finally, the photo editor can save the photo in various formats. This includes exporting the photo for use on the web, printing, or sending via email.

Photo editing can be a powerful tool for graphic designers to create stunning visuals. By understanding the different techniques used in photo editing, graphic designers can create amazing visuals that will captivate their audience.

5.2: Image Manipulation

Image manipulation is a critical component of graphic design. It involves the use of software to modify, enhance, or otherwise alter an existing image. Image manipulation techniques range from simple color adjustments to complex photo retouching.

Image manipulation is often used to improve the look of an image, or to make it look more aesthetically pleasing. It can also be used to add text, graphics, or other elements to an image, or to make an image appear larger or smaller.

In addition to the aesthetic benefits of image manipulation, it can also be used to perform basic editing tasks such as cropping, resizing, and rotating an image. It can also be used for more advanced tasks such as adding shadows or reflections, blurring or sharpening an image, and creating special effects.

When manipulating images, it is important to maintain the integrity of the original image. This means that any changes made should be subtle and should not drastically alter the overall look of the image. Additionally, it is important to use image manipulation techniques in a responsible manner, as some techniques can be used to create images that are misleading or inaccurate.

When manipulating images, it is also important to consider the file format of the image. Different file formats have different properties that affect how they can be manipulated. For example, some file formats are better suited for printing or displaying on a web page, while others are better for making small edits or adding elements to an image.

Finally, it is important to be aware of copyright and image licensing when manipulating images. Copyright laws may restrict how images can be used and manipulated, so it is important to check with the owner of the image before using or manipulating it. Additionally, some images may be subject to digital rights management (DRM), which can restrict how they can be used and manipulated.

Overall, image manipulation is an important part of graphic design. It can be used to enhance an image or to make it more aesthetically pleasing, as well as to perform basic editing tasks. It is important to maintain the integrity of the original image when manipulating it, as well as to consider the file format and copyright restrictions. By following these guidelines, graphic designers can make use of image manipulation to create stunning visuals.

5.3: Image Management

The use of images is an important part of graphic design. It is essential to properly manage the images used in any project to ensure that they are the highest quality, relevant to the project, and legal to use.

When selecting images, it is important to ensure that they are the right size and format for the project. An image that is too small or of low resolution will appear pixelated, while one that is too large may require resizing or cropping, which can affect the quality of the image.

It is also important to ensure that the image is appropriate for the project. When selecting images, consider the message that the image conveys and the audience of the project. Images should be chosen based on the context of the project and should not be offensive or inappropriate.

When using images, it is important to ensure that they are legally obtained. Some images are subject to copyright and require permission to use them. It is important to obtain the necessary permissions for any images used in a project.

Once images have been obtained, it is important to store and organize them properly. Images should be stored in a designated folder on the computer, and should be labeled clearly to make them easy to find. It is also important to keep a list or spreadsheet of any images used in a project and where they were obtained from.

Managing images effectively is an important part of graphic design. By following these guidelines, designers can ensure that the images used in their projects are of the highest quality, appropriate for the project, and legally obtained.

Chapter 6: Designing for Print

Designing for print is a process that requires a unique set of skills and knowledge. Print design differs from digital design in that it requires more attention to detail, as it will be seen in its physical form. Before starting a print design project, it is important to consider the intended outcome and audience.

When designing for print, the designer must first decide on the size of the project. This will determine the size of the paper, as well as the amount of information that can be included. They should also consider the final form of the design, such as a poster, brochure, book, or magazine.

When it comes to the design elements, the designer should consider the color scheme, fonts, images, and overall layout. Color is especially important in print design, as it can be used to create a certain mood or feeling. Choosing the right font is also important, as it must be legible and appropriate for the project. Images should be chosen carefully, as they can be used to add visual interest to the design.

When laying out the design, it is important to make sure that the content flows well and is easy to read. The designer should also consider the hierarchy of information, ensuring that the most important elements are placed at the top. They should also be aware of the bleed area, which is the area of the design that will be trimmed off when printing.

Finally, the designer should consider the printing process. Depending on the project, a designer may choose to use offset printing, digital printing, or screen printing. Each of these processes has its own advantages and disadvantages, and it is important to choose the right one based on the project's needs.

By taking all of these factors into consideration, a designer can create a stunning print design that will stand out from the crowd. With the right knowledge and attention to detail, a designer can create a piece of art that will be enjoyed for years to come.

6.1: Layout Design

Layout design is a critical component of graphic design and is the process of arranging elements on a page to create a visual design. It is an important part of any visual communication, as it helps to establish the hierarchy of the content and presents the information in an effective and attractive way.

The layout of a design should be cohesive and organized, and should be created with a clear purpose and message in mind. It should also be tailored to the target audience, as the layout will influence how the viewer perceives the content.

When designing a layout, it is important to consider the elements that will be included. These may include text, images, illustrations, diagrams, symbols, and other graphics. The layout should be organized in a way that is easy to understand and navigate. This includes making sure that the elements are arranged in a logical manner, with enough white space to provide clarity and focus.

The use of colour and typography should also be considered when designing a layout. Colour can be used to create contrast, draw attention to important elements, and add visual interest. Typography should be legible and consistent, and should be chosen to complement the design.

When creating a layout, it is also important to consider the size and scale of the elements. It is important to make sure that the elements are sized appropriately, so that they are legible and easy to read. The margin and grid should also be taken into consideration, as this will help to create a visually balanced layout.

Finally, it is important to consider the overall aesthetic of the design. The design should be unified, coherent, and aesthetically pleasing. This can be achieved through the use of consistency, symmetry, and balance in the design.

Layout design is a key part of graphic design, and it is important to understand the principles of design in order to create effective and attractive layouts. By considering the elements, colour, typography, size, scale, margin, grid, and overall aesthetic, designers can create layouts that will effectively communicate their message.

6.2: Printing Processes

Printing processes are used to create fine art prints, photographs, and other digital media. They involve a range of techniques, from traditional lithography to modern digital printing. The printing process starts with a digital file, which is then transferred to a printing plate or substrate. From there, the image is printed directly onto the substrate. Depending on the type of printing, the image is then transferred to paper, fabric, or other materials.

Traditional printing processes include lithography, letterpress, and silkscreen. Lithography involves creating a printing plate with a chemical process, which allows for accurate reproduction of an image. Letterpress printing is a relief printing technique, where raised reliefs are inked and pressed onto paper. Silkscreen printing is a stencil-based printing technique, where ink is pushed through a stencil onto the substrate.

Digital printing processes are commonly used for printing photographs and digital artwork. Digital printing is a much more efficient and cost-effective process than traditional printing processes. Digital printing processes use a variety of technologies, from inkjet to laser printing. Inkjet printing is a form of thermal printing, where ink droplets are directed onto the substrate. Laser printing uses a laser beam to form the image on the substrate.

The printing process can be a complex process, and it is important to consider a number of factors when selecting the right printing process. The type of substrate, desired image quality, cost, and turnaround time are all important factors to consider. With the right printing process, it is possible to create stunning visuals with beautiful color and detail.

6.3: Working with Printers

Working with printers can be an important part of a graphic designer's job, as it is crucial to ensure that the final product looks good and is printed correctly. Printers come in a variety of shapes and sizes, and each will require different settings and techniques to produce the best results.

When working with printers, it is important to have an understanding of the different types of printing, such as digital, offset and screen printing. Digital printing is the most common type of printing used for graphic design projects, as it is fast and relatively inexpensive. Offset printing is used for larger batches of prints, and is more expensive but produces better results. Screen printing is used for large-scale projects and can be very cost-effective for large orders.

It is also essential to understand the basics of color management when using printers. This includes understanding color theory, how to use color profiles, and the various types of color systems available. By understanding the basics of color management, designers can ensure that prints will look the same in their design as they do when printed.

Designers should also understand the various printing techniques available, such as spot colors, four-color process printing, halftone printing, and specialty printing. Each of these techniques has its own set of advantages and disadvantages, and understanding which technique is right for a particular project is key to producing a successful print.

In addition to understanding the different types of printing and color management techniques, it is also important to have an understanding of the different materials that can be used when printing. Different types of paper, cardstock, and other substrates can be used to create different effects, and understanding the qualities of each material is important to creating successful prints.

Finally, it is important to understand the basics of preparing artwork for printing. This includes understanding the process of setting up bleeds and margins, creating layouts, and creating spot color separations. Following these steps correctly will ensure that the final product looks its best and is printed correctly.

By understanding the basics of working with printers, designers can ensure that their projects look their best and are printed correctly. Knowing the different types of printing, color management techniques, materials, and artwork preparation will allow designers to produce successful prints and create stunning visuals.

Chapter 7: Web Design Fundamentals

Web design is an ever-evolving field that requires knowledge of both graphic design and coding to create stunning visuals. In this chapter, we will explore the fundamentals of web design and how it is used to create an interactive, visually appealing experience for users.

We will begin by discussing the technical aspects of web design, such as HTML and CSS. We will then discuss the different types of web design, including responsive, adaptive, and static web design. We will also discuss the importance of typography, colors, and imagery in web design.

The first aspect of web design is HTML, or Hypertext Markup Language. HTML is a coding language used to create the structure of a website. It is used to create the different elements of a website, such as navigation, headings, and paragraphs. HTML is also used to create hyperlinks, which allow users to navigate from one page to another.

CSS, or Cascading Style Sheets, is the language used to add styling to HTML elements. CSS is used to control the positioning, size, font, and color of HTML elements. It is also used to create animations and transitions, which can enhance the user experience on a website.

Responsive web design is a technique used to create sites that can adjust to different screen sizes and devices. Responsive web design ensures that a website looks good and functions properly on any device, including mobile devices.

Adaptive web design is a technique used to create sites that can adjust to different devices and screen sizes, but with limited functionality. Adaptive web design is used when a website needs to be optimized for specific devices, such as a tablet or smartphone.

Static web design is a technique used to create websites with fixed elements. It is used when a website does not need to be optimized for different devices, such as a portfolio website or a basic information website.

Typography is an important aspect of web design. It is used to create a hierarchy of text, which makes it easier for users to read and understand the information presented. Typography can also be used to create an aesthetic for a website, as the font used can drastically change the overall look and feel of a website.

Colors are also an important element of web design. Colors can be used to create an aesthetic for a website, as well as to convey a certain message or emotion. Careful selection of colors is essential for creating a visually appealing experience for users.

Finally, imagery is an important element of web design. Images can be used to draw attention to certain elements, as well as to create an aesthetic for the website. Careful selection of images is essential for creating a visually appealing experience for users.

In this chapter, we have explored the fundamentals of web design. Web design is an ever-evolving field that requires knowledge of both graphic design and coding to create stunning visuals. By understanding the technical aspects of web design, as well as the importance of typography, colors, and imagery, designers can create an interactive, visually appealing experience for users.

7.1: Page Layout Design

Page layout design is a key component of graphic design. It involves the organization of elements such as text, images, and shapes on a page in order to create a visually pleasing and effective design. Creating a page layout design requires an understanding of composition, typography, and color theory.

The first step in creating a page layout design is to determine the purpose of the design. This will help guide the layout and design decisions that are made. When creating a design, it is important to consider the audience and the intended message that is being communicated. This will help ensure that the design is effective in conveying the intended message.

Once the purpose of the design has been determined, the next step is to consider the composition. This involves arranging elements such as images, text, and shapes on the page in a balanced and attractive way. Good composition can help create an effective design that is visually pleasing.

The next step is to consider the typography. Typography involves the selection and arrangement of typefaces, font sizes, and other typographic elements. The right font choice and arrangement of type can help create a design that is both visually appealing and easy to read.

The final step in creating a page layout design is to consider the use of color. Color theory can help create a design that is visually appealing and effective in conveying the intended message. Using color effectively can also help create a sense of balance and harmony in the design.

Creating a page layout design requires an understanding of composition, typography, and color theory. It is important to consider the purpose of the design, composition, typography, and color when creating a page layout design. By considering these elements, a designer can create a design that is visually pleasing and effective in conveying the intended message.

7.2: Coding Basics

Coding is an essential part of graphic design and it can be quite intimidating for those new to the craft. For those starting out, it is important to understand the basics of coding in order to create stunning visuals. This will provide an overview of coding and its fundamentals.

A fundamental concept in coding is the idea of syntax. Syntax is the structure of a program, and it is important to understand the basic syntax for the language you are coding in. Syntax includes elements like variables, statements, and operators, which are the building blocks of a program. Variables store values and can be used to represent data. Statements are instructions that tell the program to do something. Operators are symbols that are used to compare, modify, or calculate values.

Another important concept in coding is the concept of data types. Data types are categories of data that tell the program how to interpret it. The most common data types are integers, strings, and booleans. Integers are whole numbers, strings are pieces of text, and booleans are true or false values. Understanding the different data types is essential to writing code.

Functions are also important in coding. Functions allow you to group several instructions together into one piece of code. This makes it easier to organize your code and helps you avoid repeating code. Functions can be used to perform calculations, manipulate data, and more.

It is also important to understand the concept of loops. Loops allow you to repeat a set of instructions a certain number of times. This makes it easy to perform repetitive tasks without having to write out the instructions each time.

Finally, it is important to understand the concept of debugging. Debugging is the process of finding and fixing errors in a program. Debugging can be done manually, or with the help of a debugger. Debugging is an essential skill for any programmer and is critical for creating reliable and efficient code.

By understanding the basics of coding, such as syntax, data types, functions, loops, and debugging, one can create stunning visuals with ease. With the right understanding and practice, coding can be a powerful tool for graphic designers.

7.3: Designing for Mobile

Mobile design has become increasingly important in the world of graphic design. Mobile devices come in all shapes and sizes, and designers must consider how their designs will look on devices of all sizes, as well as how users interact with them. Designers must also consider how their designs will look on different operating systems.

When designing for mobile, the most important factor is to keep the design clean and uncluttered. Designers should focus on the essential elements of their design and remove anything that does not contribute to the overall goal. Ensure that the design is easy to read and navigate on a small screen. This includes clear, legible typography and simple navigation. Consider how the design will flow between different devices and how it will look on different operating systems.

Designers should also consider how users interact with their design on mobile devices. Mobile devices are typically used with a single finger, so designers should consider the size of buttons and other interactive elements. Designers should also consider the user's environment when designing for mobile. Mobile users often use their devices while on the go, so designs should be optimized for quick and easy use.

When designing for mobile, it is important to consider the device's capabilities. Some mobile devices have limited memory, so it is important to keep the design as lightweight as possible. Designers should also consider the device's battery life when designing for mobile. Mobile devices are often used for extended periods of time, so designers should create designs that are efficient and conserve battery life.

Designers should also consider the different resolutions that mobile devices have. Mobile devices have varying screen sizes and resolutions, so designers should create designs that are optimized for all resolutions. Designers should also consider how the design will look when viewed on different operating systems.

In conclusion, designing for mobile is a complex and challenging process. Designers must consider the device's capabilities, how users interact with their design, and how the design will look on different operating systems. By considering these factors, designers can create designs that are optimized for mobile devices and provide users with an enjoyable experience.

Chapter 8: Creating Motion Graphics

Motion graphics is a form of visual communication that combines text, audio, and moving imagery to create a powerful story. Motion graphics have become an increasingly popular tool for designers to create engaging visuals that capture the attention of viewers. They can be used to create stunning graphics for video projects, websites, and other forms of media.

Creating motion graphics can be a complex process, however, it can be broken down into several key components. The first step is creating the storyboard, which is the blueprint for the motion graphics project. This includes outlining the visuals, choosing the colors, and deciding how the elements will move and interact with one another. Once the storyboard is complete, the designer can begin to create the motion graphics. This includes adding elements such as text, logos, and animation to the project.

The next step is to create the animation, which is the movement of the elements in the motion graphics. This can be done using various software applications such as Flash, After Effects, and 3D modeling. Animating the elements can be a complex process, but by understanding the fundamentals of animation, a designer can create great looking motion graphics.

The final step is to add sound to the motion graphics. This can be done by adding background music or sound effects to enhance the visuals. By creating soundscapes, a designer can create a powerful moment for viewers as they experience the visuals.

Creating motion graphics can be a complex process, but it is an important skill for any designer to have. By understanding the fundamentals of design, animation, and sound, a designer can create beautiful and engaging visuals that will capture the attention of the viewers. With the right tools and techniques, a designer can create stunning motion graphics for any project.

8.1: Animation Principles

Animation is a powerful visual tool that can be used to create stunning visuals in graphic design. It involves the use of motion to bring an image to life, adding depth and dimension to otherwise static images. Animation can be used to bring an idea or concept to life, by incorporating movement and interactive elements.

The principles of animation are an important part of creating effective visuals. The 12 principles of animation, developed by Walt Disney's legendary animators Ollie Johnston and Frank Thomas, outline the fundamentals of animation. They are: squash and stretch, anticipation, slow in and slow out, arcs, timing and spacing, staging, follow through and overlapping action, straight ahead action and pose to pose, exaggeration, solid drawing, appeal, and secondary action.

Squash and stretch is the idea that an object can be deformed to enhance the illusion of movement. This is done by stretching or squashing an object when it moves or changes direction. Anticipation is the idea that a character or object will prepare for an action before actually performing it. This can be done through body language or other visual cues. Slow in and slow out involves gradually increasing or decreasing a movement over a period of time, to create a more natural and realistic movement.

Arcs refer to the idea that most natural movements follow an arc shape, rather than a straight line. Timing and spacing involve the idea that movement should be consistent. Staging is the process of setting the scene and presenting a concept in a clear and effective way. Follow through and overlapping action refers to the idea that objects, such as hair or clothing, should move with the character's movements.

Straight ahead action and pose to pose involve the idea that animation can be created in two ways. Straight ahead action is when the animator draws each frame one after the other, from beginning to end. Pose to pose involves the animator drawing key frames, then filling in the frames between each key frame. Exaggeration is the idea of exaggerating certain elements to add emphasis and create a more interesting visual. Solid drawing refers to the idea of creating a solid foundation for the animation, with a strong sense of weight and proportion.

Appeal is the idea that a character should be visually appealing and have a unique personality. Secondary action involves creating action that occurs in the background, to add depth and realism to the animation. By following these principles, animation can be used to create stunning visuals in graphic design.

8.2: Types of Animation

Animation is an incredibly powerful medium to create stunning visuals. There are a variety of types of animation, each with their own unique style and capabilities. From hand-drawn 2D animations to 3D computer-generated animations, there is something for everyone. In this subchapter, we will explore the different types of animation available.

2D Animation

2D animation is often referred to as traditional animation. This type of animation is created by hand-drawing each frame of a scene and then piecing them together to create a continuous loop. The most common type of 2D animation is cel animation, which is created by drawing characters and objects on transparent sheets of plastic.

3D Animation

3D animation is created using computer-generated models and is often referred to as computer-generated imagery (CGI). This type of animation offers a greater level of realism and depth compared to 2D animation. It is often used in movies, video games, and other forms of digital media.

Stop-Motion Animation

Stop-motion animation is a type of animation that is created by taking a series of photographs of objects or characters and then piecing them together to create a continuous loop. This type of animation is often used in claymation or puppet shows.

Whiteboard Animation

Whiteboard animation is a type of animation that is created by drawing on a whiteboard or other flat surface. This type of animation is used to explain complex topics or provide a narrative for storytelling.

Motion Graphics

Motion graphics is a type of animation that is used to create titles, logos, and other graphical elements. This type of animation is often used for branding and marketing purposes.

Cutout Animation

Cutout animation is a type of animation that is created by cutting out physical objects and then animating them. This type of animation is often used in children's shows or educational videos.

Rotoscoping

Rotoscoping is a type of animation that is created by tracing over live-action footage. This technique is often used to create realistic looking animated characters.

Vector Animation

Vector animation is a type of animation that is created using vector graphics. This type of animation is often used for cartoons and video games due to its scalability and flexibility.

These are just some of the many types of animation available for creating stunning visuals. Each one has its own unique style and capabilities, so it's important to consider which type of animation is best suited to your project.

8.3: Motion Graphics Techniques

Motion graphics are an essential element of modern graphic design, allowing designers to create dynamic visuals that draw the attention of viewers. This will discuss the various techniques and tools used to create motion graphics in a professional setting.

First, it is important to understand the basics of motion graphics. Motion graphics are composed of various elements such as shapes, text, and images that are animated to create a visually stimulating piece. They can be used to convey a message, create a narrative, or simply provide an aesthetic. To create successful motion graphics, designers must have an understanding of animation principles such as timing, motion paths, and easing.

Next, designers must consider the tools they will use to create their motion graphics. Popular software such as Adobe After Effects and Cinema 4D are widely used in the industry for creating motion graphics. These programs provide a range of features and tools that allow designers to create high quality motion graphics quickly and efficiently.

Once the tools are chosen, designers must consider the techniques they will use to create their motion graphics. These techniques include keyframing, motion tracking, and rotoscoping. Keyframing is the process of setting key frames at specific points in time and adjusting the values of those frames to create a smooth animation. Motion tracking is used to align an object with a moving element in the scene. Rotoscoping involves tracing over live-action footage to create a more realistic animation.

Finally, designers must consider the style of the motion graphics they are creating. Styles such as kinetic typography, 3D animation, and kinetic illustration can be used to create unique visuals. Each style has its own set of techniques and tools that must be mastered in order to achieve the desired result.

By mastering the techniques and tools used in motion graphics, designers can create stunning visuals that captivate viewers and draw them into the story. With the right knowledge and understanding, designers can create visually stunning motion graphics that will make an impact on viewers.

Chapter 9: Brand Identity Design

Creating a successful brand identity is essential to the success of a business. A brand identity is the visual embodiment of a company's values, mission, and personality. It is the face of a company, representing who they are and what they stand for. It is also an essential part of any branding and marketing campaign.

In this chapter, we will discuss the importance of branding and identity design, the basics of creating a successful brand identity, and the design elements of a strong brand identity. We will also explore the tools and techniques used in creating a memorable and effective brand identity.

Brand identity begins with establishing a brand strategy. This involves researching the company, its target audience, and their industry. This research helps to identify the company's mission, values, and goals. It is important to understand the company's strengths and weaknesses, as well as its competition. This information will help to create an effective brand identity that sets the company apart from its competition.

Once the brand strategy is established, it is time to begin the design process. This involves creating a logo, developing a color palette, and selecting typography. The logo is the cornerstone of the brand identity, and it should be carefully crafted to convey the company's message and personality. The color palette should be chosen to reflect the company's values and mission. Typography should be selected to express the company's personality and to be legible and aesthetically pleasing.

The next step is to create a brand guidelines document. This document should include all the elements of the brand identity, such as the logo, color palette, typography, and imagery. It should also provide guidance on how to use the brand identity elements and provide examples of how to apply them to different media.

Once the brand identity is created, it is important to ensure that it is used consistently across all media. This includes print, digital, and environmental elements. Consistent use of the brand identity helps to ensure that the brand is recognizable and memorable.

Finally, it is important to measure the success of the brand identity. This can be done by tracking metrics such as brand recognition and message recall. This information can help to identify any areas where the brand identity needs to be improved and provide insights into how the brand identity can be used more effectively.

In conclusion, creating a successful brand identity is essential for any business. It is important to understand the company's mission, values, and goals and to use this information to create a strong brand identity. Brand identity design involves creating a logo, color palette, typography, and imagery. It is also important to create a brand guidelines document and ensure that the brand identity is used consistently across all media. Finally, it is important to measure the success of the brand identity to ensure that it is effective.

9.1: Logo Design

Logo design is an essential part of any graphic design project. It is a graphical representation of a company, organization, or individual that is used to promote recognition and brand identity. Whether you're a professional graphic designer or a novice, there are a few important elements you should keep in mind when creating a logo design.

The first step is to identify the purpose of the logo. What message are you trying to convey? Is the logo meant to represent a company or product? This will help you decide what type of logo you should create.

The next step is to consider the target audience. Who will be viewing the logo? Is it intended for a specific age group or demographic? Taking the time to consider the target audience will help ensure that your logo design resonates with the correct audience.

The third step is to consider the shape, size, and colors of the logo. Choose a shape that is appropriate for the logo's purpose. Consider the size of the logo and the colors that will be used. These elements should be chosen carefully in order to ensure that the logo design is effective.

The fourth step is to create a concept. This is the most important part of the logo design process. Take the time to brainstorm ideas and come up with a concept that is unique and memorable. This is also the best time to consider any fonts and other design elements that will be used in your logo.

Finally, once the concept is finalized, it's time to create the final logo. This involves using software such as Adobe Photoshop or Illustrator to bring the concept to life. Take the time to create a logo that is unique and visually appealing.

Logo design is an important part of any graphic design project. Taking the time to follow the steps discussed above will help ensure that your logo design is successful.

9.2: Developing a Brand

Developing a brand is an integral part of graphic design. A brand is a recognizable and consistent identity that sets a business or organization apart from its competitors. It is essential for any business or organization to create a unique and memorable brand identity which will give customers a sense of trust and recognition.

Designers play a huge role in developing a strong brand identity. The visual elements of a brand, such as logos, colors, typography, and imagery, are all important elements to consider when designing a brand. Logos are often the most recognizable part of a brand, so it is important to create a design that is unique and memorable. Colors are also an important element to consider when creating a brand identity, as colors can evoke certain emotions and feelings. Typography is another important element to consider when designing a brand, as it can be used to communicate an organization's message in a powerful way. Imagery is also important, as it can help to communicate the brand's message in a visually appealing way.

When developing a brand, it is important to consider the target audience. It is essential to create a design that resonates with the target audience and communicates the brand's message in a way that appeals to them. Knowing the target audience's age, gender, and interests can help to create a design that is specifically tailored to them.

It is also important to consider the brand's values and mission when creating a brand identity. A brand's values and mission can help to create a design that is consistent and reflects the brand's core beliefs.

Finally, it is important to consider the brand's tone of voice. The tone of voice should be consistent throughout all communication, from website copy to social media posts. This will help to create a unified and recognizable brand experience that customers will recognize and trust.

Developing a brand is an important part of graphic design, and designers play a crucial role in creating a strong and recognizable brand identity. It is essential to consider the target audience, the brand's values and mission, and the brand's tone of voice when creating a brand identity. By following these steps, designers can create a unique and powerful brand identity that will help to set a business or organization apart from its competitors.

9.3: Creating a Brand Guidelines

Creating a brand guidelines is an essential step for any business, as it sets the standard for how the company's brand should be presented to the public. A brand guidelines document defines the basic rules of how to use logos, typography, color, imagery, and other elements that reflect the brand's identity.

When creating a brand guidelines, the first step is to establish the brand's identity. This includes the company's mission, values, and personality. Once these elements are established, it's time to create the visual representation of the brand. This is done by designing the company's logo, typography, color palette, and other visual elements that communicate the brand's identity.

Once the visual elements are established, it's time to create the guidelines that will govern how they should be used. This includes defining the rules for how to use the logo, typography, color, and other elements in all types of media, from print to digital. It should also include guidelines for how to use the brand's identity in other contexts, such as on packaging and promotional materials.

When defining the guidelines for how to use the brand's identity, it's important to be consistent and clear. This means that the rules should be specific about what is and isn't allowed, and they should be applied consistently across all mediums. It's also important to ensure that the brand's identity is used correctly, and that it's not used in a way that would be damaging to the company's reputation.

It's also important to make sure that the brand's identity is protected. This means that any unauthorized use of the brand's identity should be prevented. This includes using the logo, typography, color, and other elements without permission.

Creating a brand guidelines document is essential for any business, as it sets the standard for how the company's brand should be represented. By establishing the brand's identity, defining the rules for how the brand's identity should be used, and protecting the brand's identity, companies can ensure that their brand is presented in the best way possible.

Chapter 10: Professional Practices and Ethics

Graphic design is a field that requires a great deal of skill, knowledge, and creativity. Because of this, it is important for graphic designers to follow professional practices and ethics in order to produce high-quality work. Professionalism is a must when dealing with clients, colleagues, and other stakeholders in the design process. It is important to always be mindful of the client's needs and wants, as well as any deadlines or other expectations that have been set.

It is also essential to maintain a level of professionalism when it comes to communication. This includes being respectful and courteous in all interactions, as well as being open to criticism and feedback. It is also important to be honest and transparent about any mistakes or issues that may arise during the design process.

In addition to professionalism, there are certain ethical considerations that must be taken into account when creating graphic design work. It is important to be aware of copyright laws and regulations, as well as any moral or ethical implications that may arise from the design work. It is also important to be aware of any cultural or social implications of the design work, as this can have a large impact on the success of the project.

It is also important to stay up-to-date on the latest trends and techniques in the design industry. By staying informed, graphic designers can ensure that their work is of the highest quality and that it is engaging and visually appealing. They should also be aware of any new technologies or software that may be relevant to their work.

Finally, it is important to maintain a good reputation as a graphic designer. This includes being reliable and dependable, as well as being open to feedback and criticism from clients and colleagues. It is important to take responsibility for any mistakes or issues that may arise, and to strive to always produce high-quality work.

By following these practices and ethics, graphic designers can ensure that their work is of the highest quality and that they are respected and valued in the design industry. It is essential to be honest, transparent, and professional at all times, and to always strive for excellence in the work that is produced.

10.1: Working with Clients

Graphic design professionals must develop effective relationships with clients to ensure successful outcomes. The key to successful client relationships is communication. It is important to provide clear and concise communication throughout the project, discussing the project goals, overall look and feel, and any budget constraints that should be taken into consideration. It is also important to discuss deadlines and milestones to ensure the project is completed on time.

Once a client has been identified, the graphic designer must be prepared to listen to the client's ideas and needs. The designer must also be prepared to ask questions and offer feedback and suggestions. This dialogue helps to ensure that the client understands the project goals and that the designer understands the client's vision.

To maintain a successful working relationship, the graphic designer must be responsive to the client's questions and concerns. It is important to be available to the client and respond to communications in a timely manner. This is especially important when the project deadlines are tight.

The graphic designer should also be prepared to make adjustments to the project as needed. It is important to be flexible in order to meet the client's needs. This not only shows that the designer is willing to work with the client to achieve the desired results, but also shows that the designer is able to adjust the project to fit the client's budget.

Finally, the graphic designer should provide feedback to the client throughout the project. This feedback helps to ensure that the client is satisfied with the end result. It also provides the designer with an opportunity to adjust the project as needed to meet the client's vision.

Overall, it is important for graphic designers to develop successful client relationships. Clear and concise communication, responsiveness, flexibility, and feedback are all essential components of successful client relationships. Working collaboratively with clients helps to ensure that a successful outcome is achieved.

10.2: Understanding Copyright

Copyright is an important aspect of graphic design. It is essential for protecting the intellectual property of an individual or organization. Having a solid understanding of copyright laws can help designers create visuals without infringement.

Copyright law grants exclusive rights to creators of original works. This includes books, music, videos, photographs, and other artistic works. Copyright laws protect the work from unauthorized use by others. To establish copyright protection, the work must be original and fixed in a tangible form.

When a work is copyrighted, it is protected from being copied, distributed, or altered without the permission of the owner. This includes reproducing the work either in its entirety or in part. It also includes creating a derivative work based on the original work.

To use copyrighted material legally, designers must obtain permission from the copyright holder. This permission is usually given in the form of a license. Licenses can restrict the use of content to a certain number of copies, limit the type of use, or require a fee for each use.

Designers should also be aware of the concept of fair use. Fair use is a legal doctrine that allows limited use of copyrighted material without permission from the copyright holder. This includes criticism, comment, news reporting, teaching, scholarship, and research. Fair use is determined on a case-by-case basis and is based on four factors: the purpose and character of the use, the nature of the copyrighted work, the amount used, and the effect on the potential market for the work.

Designers should also be familiar with the Creative Commons license. This license allows for free use of copyrighted material, as long as the user follows the terms and conditions defined in the license. Creative Commons licenses are used to provide open access to copyrighted works and allow for reuse or remixing.

Understanding copyright is an important part of becoming a successful graphic designer. Knowing the rules and regulations can help designers create stunning visuals without infringing on the rights of others. By familiarizing themselves with copyright laws, designers can create unique and innovative works that are legally protected.

10.3: Professional Standards

Graphic design is a highly creative field that requires the utmost professionalism from its practitioners. It is important to remember that professional standards must always be adhered to in order to produce high-quality work.

To ensure that professional standards are met, designers should develop an understanding of the industry's best practices. This should include knowledge of the latest software, technologies, and tools that are available. Additionally, designers should stay up-to-date with the industry's trends and regulations to ensure that they are creating work that is in line with the latest standards.

Designers should also be mindful of the ethical aspects of their work. For instance, they should avoid plagiarism and copyright infringement. Additionally, designers should ensure that their work reflects only their own thoughts and ideas and that they are not attempting to copy someone else's work.

Designers should also be aware of the importance of effective communication. They should strive to communicate their ideas and deliverables clearly to their clients. Additionally, designers should be open to feedback and willing to make adjustments as needed to ensure that their clients are satisfied with the final product.

Finally, designers should maintain a high level of professionalism at all times. This means that they should be punctual, reliable, and respectful to their clients and colleagues. Additionally, designers should be willing to go the extra mile to ensure that their work meets the highest standards and that their clients are happy with the results.

By adhering to these professional standards, designers can ensure that they are producing quality work that is in line with the industry's best practices. Additionally, they can maintain strong relationships with their clients and colleagues and ensure that their work is as successful as possible.

Chapter 11: Conclusion

Graphic design has become an integral part of our lives. It helps to communicate information visually and can be used to create stunning visuals. Through the use of color, texture, typography, and imagery, designers can create artwork that conveys a message and catches the eye.

In this book, we discussed the fundamentals of graphic design, including the basics of color theory, typography, and composition. We also explored the importance of layout and how to use shapes and lines to create a cohesive design. We discussed the advantages of different software programs and established best practices for creating effective visuals.

Graphic design is a skill that requires practice and dedication. It takes time and effort to become proficient, and even then, it's a continuous learning process. However, with the right tools and knowledge, anyone can create stunning visuals.

Graphic design is a powerful tool and a great way to express yourself. It can be used to tell stories, evoke emotions, and communicate information. With the right techniques, anyone can create beautiful visuals that capture the attention of an audience.

Creating a successful design requires careful consideration and planning. It's important to think about the purpose of the design, the audience, and the message you're trying to convey. Once you understand these elements, you can create visuals that will stand out and engage your audience.

Graphic design is an art form that takes time and practice to master. There is no one-size-fits-all approach to creating visuals and the best designs come from experimentation and creativity. Keep exploring and experimenting with different tools and techniques to find the best way to express your ideas.

Graphic design is a rewarding and exciting field. With the right tools and knowledge, you can create stunning visuals and tell powerful stories. This book provided an introduction to the fundamentals of graphic design and the techniques used to create beautiful visuals. With the right approach, anyone can create stunning visuals that capture the attention of their audience.

Made in United States
Troutdale, OR
07/01/2023